Chapter one

Georgie Brown finished washing her dad's car and went into the house.

"Dad, I've finished. Can I have my money now?"

Georgie's dad went outside to look at the car. Georgie followed him. Her dad walked all round the car and then bent down to look at the wheels. At last he nodded.

"You've done a really good job here, Georgie," he said. "You have washed the car six times so here is a pound."

"Thanks, Dad."

Georgie took the pound note and went up to her bedroom. She took out her red moneybox and opened it. It was full of money. Georgie had spent the last few weeks washing people's cars. She was saving up to buy a model helicopter. Georgie took all of the money out of the box and put it into her pocket. It was very heavy.

"I think it's time to take this lot to the post office," she said.

Georgie Brown
and the
Pound Notes

Stan Cullimore

Georgie went down
to the front door.

"Dad?"

Her dad put his head round the kitchen door.

"Yes!"

Georgie put on her coat.

"I'm going to the post office."

"OK," said Dad. "Be careful when you cross
the road."

"Dad, I'm always careful," said Georgie.
"I'm not a little kid any more."

With that, she went out of the house and
set off towards the post office.

Chapter Two

When Georgie got to the post office she was glad to see that it was almost empty. She didn't like waiting in line, it was boring. She went up to the counter. A girl was sitting behind the glass. She was writing numbers down in a book.

"Hello," said Georgie, "I want to pay some money in, please."

The girl looked up and smiled.

"Hello, Georgie."

She put down her pen and watched as Georgie pushed her money under the glass.

"Did you save all this from your pocket money, Georgie?" asked the girl.

Georgie shook her head.

"No, I've been washing people's cars as well."

"Well, you must be good at it, if people are paying you all this money," said the girl. "I might ask you to wash my car the next time it gets dirty."

Georgie smiled.

"I'd love to. I'm saving up to buy a model helicopter and they cost a lot."

The girl started to count the money that Georgie had given her. Georgie turned away and looked around the post office.

"Er, Georgie?" It was the girl.

Georgie turned back to look at her.

"Yes?"

"I've got bad news for you," said the girl.

Chapter Three

"What is it?" asked Georgie.

"If you just go and sit down over there, I'll send the manager out to talk to you," said the girl. "He will be able to tell you more about it."

Georgie went and sat down. She did not know what to think. What on earth could the bad news be? A moment later, the door behind him opened and the manager came out.

"Georgie, can you come into my office?" he asked.

Georgie went into the office. The manager closed the door.

"Jane tells me that you have been washing people's cars."

Georgie nodded.

"That's right."

"How much do you charge?" asked the manager.

Georgie smiled. So that was it! The manager wanted Georgie to wash his car. That wasn't such bad news.

"Well, I don't charge much. But I'll do yours if you like."

The manager smiled.

"That's very kind of you, Georgie. But that is not why I wanted to talk to you."

He held up a pound note.

"Was this pound note in the money you just gave to Jane?"

Georgie nodded.

"I'm sorry to say that it isn't a real pound note – it's a fake."

Chapter Four

Georgie shook her head.

"It isn't fair. I worked really hard at washing those cars. But someone has given me a pound note that isn't real. So now it isn't worth any money?"

The manager nodded.

Georgie was silent for a moment. The manager went over to her.

"Don't worry," he said. "You are not the only one who has been given one of these. There are lots of them about at the moment. The police think that someone around here is making them and giving them to people."

"But the good news is that you may be able to help us catch this person."

Georgie looked up.

"How?"

"Well, the police think that the person who is making these fake notes lives in your road. If you can tell us who gave you this pound note, we will have found them!"

Georgie nodded.

"That's easy. It was ..." Georgie stopped.

"It was who?" asked the manager.

Georgie gulped. She sat down and put her head in her hands.

"It was my dad," she said sadly.

"Oh, dear," said the manager.

Chapter Five

A lot of things happened in the next few minutes. The manager went into another room. He came back with two policemen. They asked Georgie who had given her the fake pound note and wrote down what she said.

After this, the policemen asked Georgie to get into the car with them. They drove to Georgie's house.

"What happens to people who make fake pound notes?" Georgie asked. "Do they go to prison?"

The policemen both nodded.

When they got to Georgie's house, the two policemen knocked on the door. Georgie's dad opened it.

"Hello, Georgie."

Then he saw the policemen and his face dropped.

"What has happened?" he asked.

"Can we come in, sir?" asked one of the policemen.

"Yes, please do." Georgie's dad let the policemen in. He took them into the kitchen. One of the policemen took out a book and started to write things down in it.

"Can I look at your wallet please, sir?" said the other policeman.

Dad looked puzzled but he took his wallet out of his pocket and handed it to the policeman.

"Thank you very much, sir."

The policeman opened the wallet and looked inside. There were some notes in the wallet. The policeman pulled them out and put them onto the table. Two of them were pound notes. The policeman held them up and looked at them carefully. He shook his head.

"These are not real," he said. "They are both fakes."

Chapter Six

Dad looked very puzzled.

"Fake notes. Are you sure?"

The policeman nodded.

Georgie sat down at the table.

"So was the one you gave to me for washing your car, Dad."

Dad looked at Georgie.

"I'm sorry, Georgie."

Georgie gulped.

"So is it true then, Dad?"

Dad sat down at the table.

"Is what true?"

Georgie looked over at her father.

"The police said that someone in this road has been making fake pound notes. They said that it could be the person who gave me the fake note."

Dad did not say anything for a long time.
Then at last he nodded.

"I think it may well be true, Georgie."
He laughed and shook his head.

"Dad, it's not funny,"
said Georgie.
"You could go to
 prison for this!"

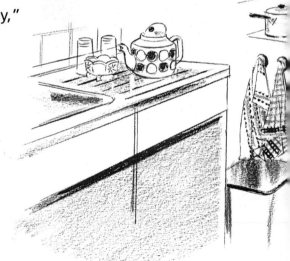

Dad stopped laughing.

"What are you talking about?"

One of the policemen nodded.

"The girl is right, sir. People who make fake bank notes do get sent to prison."

Dad nodded.

"I know they do. But it wasn't me that made the fake notes."

The policeman who was writing things down looked up.

"Then who was it?"

Chapter Seven

"I don't know who made the fake notes,"
said Dad. "But it wasn't me. I don't know
how to make them."

"Someone who lives in our road does,"
said Georgie. She frowned. "Where did
you get those pound notes from, Dad?"

Her Dad thought for a moment. He shook his
head. "I can't remember." Suddenly he
stopped. "Wait a minute.
Yes, I remember now.
It was Mr Crabtree."

"Why did he give them to you, Dad?" asked Georgie.

"I owed him two pounds. But when I saw him this morning I only had a five-pound note in my wallet. I gave him the five-pound note and he gave me those three fake pound notes as change."

Dad shook his head.

"I didn't even look at them before I put them into my wallet."

The policeman sitting at the table stood up.

"Where does this Mr Crabtree live, please, sir?"

Dad pointed out of the kitchen window.

"Next door."

Chapter Eight

The police talked to Mr Crabtree and he showed them where he made the fake pound notes. Some time later there was a knock on Georgie's front door.

Georgie opened the door. There was a policeman standing outside.

"I heard you are saving up for a model helicopter," he said. "Is that right?"

Georgie nodded.

"Well, I can't help you there," said the policeman. "But how would you like a ride in a police helicopter as a reward for helping us find Mr Crabtree?"

Georgie smiled.

"That would be just perfect, thanks. Just as long as it is not a fake helicopter!"